■SCHOLASTIC

Handwriting Practice
JOKES & RIDDLES

By Violet Findley

New York • Toronto • London • Auckland • Sydney
Mexico City • New Delhi • Hong Kong • Buenos Aires

Contents

Introduction 3

Using This Resource 4

Making a Joke & Riddle Booklet 4

Meeting the K–2 Language Arts Standards 4

Uppercase Practice Page 5

Lowercase Practice Page 6

Joke & Riddle Practice Pages 7

Blank Booklet Page 47

Booklet Cover 48

Cover design by Radames Espinoza
Interior design by Maria Lilja
Illustrations by Doug Jones

ISBN: 978-0-545-22753-7

13 14 15   40   22 21 20 19 18 17

Introduction

Welcome to *Handwriting Practice: Jokes & Riddles*! In the hustle and bustle of a hectic school day, handwriting often gets short shrift. With reading, writing, math, science, and social studies to learn, few students have the time or inclination to perfect the fine art of crossing *t*'s and dotting *i*'s. What a shame! Clear handwriting is one of the best tools available to kids for expressing big ideas and showing what they know.

That's where these lively practice pages come in! In as little as five minutes a day, you can spur students to spruce up their handwriting. Just reproduce and pass out a page, then sit back and watch kids move their pencils with levity and care. Why? Because the simple act of rewriting an amusing joke or riddle motivates them to master the shape, size, and spacing of model manuscript.

And here's more good news: The completed practice pages can be quickly bound into instant joke-and-riddle books to share with family and friends. Can you think of a cooler way to showcase a child's printing? I can't.

Read on to discover more tips for using this resource to improve your students' handwriting and, in so doing, their essential communication skills.

Your partner in education,

Violet Findley

Using This Resource

This book has been designed for easy use. Before embarking on the joke and riddle pages, it's a good idea to review the basics. Do so by distributing the upper- and lowercase practice pages to students. These sheets include arrows showing the standard way to form each letter. As students complete these pages, circulate around the room looking for writing "red flags"—that is, kids who are forming their letters in nonstandard ways, for example from the bottom up. If you notice an error, approach the student and model standard formation. This will help students rewire their handwriting habits, which will improve both the clarity and speed of their printing down the road.

Once students have reviewed the basics, they're ready to enjoy the joke and riddle pages. These pages can be reproduced in any sequence you choose. Here are some simple routines for sharing them:

Handwriting Starters Place a practice page on each student's desk for them to complete first thing in the morning.

Handwriting Center Stock a table with a "practice page of the day" for students to complete independently.

Handwriting Homework Send home a page each night for students to complete in addition to the rest of their homework.

Handwriting Folders Create personal handwriting folders filled with photocopies of the pages for students to complete at their own pace.

Making a Joke & Riddle Booklet

Once students have completed their pages, they can follow these simple directions to make personal booklets. Note: The booklets can comprise as many pages as you like. They need not include every page.

1. Cut the pages along the dashed lines, discarding the top portions.

2. Optional: Photocopy the blank booklet sheet on page 47 to add original jokes and riddles to the booklet.

3. Photocopy the booklet cover on page 48.

4. Place the booklet cover on top of the stacked pages in any order you choose.

5. Staple the book along the left-hand side.

6. Color the booklet covers and interior pages.

7. Share the booklet with family and friends.

Meeting the K–2 Language Arts Standards

Standard 3. Uses grammatical and mechanical conventions in written compositions

Uses conventions of print in writing (e.g., forms letters in print, uses upper- and lowercase letters of the alphabet, spaces words and sentences, writes from left to right and top to bottom, includes margins)

Source: *Content Knowledge: A Compendium of Standards and Benchmarks for PreK–12 Education* (4ᵗʰ Edition). (Mid-Continent Regional Educational Laboratory, 2004)

Practice Page
Uppercase Letters

Name _____

A B C D E F G H I J K L M
N O P Q R S T U V W X Y Z

Tip: Look at the arrows to see how to form each letter.

Use your best handwriting to copy each letter below.

Ha! • Ha! • Ha! • Ha! • Ha! • Ha! • Ha! • Ha!

Practice Page
Lowercase Letters

Tip: Look at the arrows to see how to form each letter.

Name _____

a b c d e f g h i j k l m n

o p q r s t u v w x y z

Use your best handwriting to copy each letter below.

Ha! • Ha! • Ha! • Ha! • Ha! • Ha! • Ha! •

Bonus chuckle!

What do you get when you cross a porcupine with a balloon?

Pop!

Practice Page 1

Name: Charlie

Use your best handwriting to copy the words.

dogs _____

cats _____

you _____

Use your best handwriting to copy the sentences below.

Why should you stay inside when it is raining cats and dogs?

Because you might step in a poodle!

Tip: Begin letters from the top, not the bottom.

Ha! • Ha! • Ha! • Ha! • Ha! • Ha!

Why should you stay
inside When it's raining
cats and dogs?

Because you might step
in a poodle!

Bonus Chuckle!

Why do dogs always run in circles?

Because it's hard to run in squares!

Tip: Pull the pencil toward the middle of your body when you write.

Name _____

Use your best handwriting to copy the words.

kitten   glass   of

Use your best handwriting to copy the sentences below.

What happened to the kitten that drank a big glass of lemonade? She became a real sourpuss!

Ha! · Ha! · Ha! · Ha! · Ha! · Ha! · Ha!

What happened to the kitten that Drank a Big Glass of lemonade, She Became a real sourpuss

Name _____

Use your best handwriting to copy the words.

gray　　　and

slipper

Use your best handwriting to copy the sentences below.

What is gray, weighs five thousand pounds, and wears a dainty glass slipper? Cinderelephant!

Ha! Ha! Ha! Ha! Ha! Ha! Ha!

What is gray, Weighs
five thousand pounds,
and wears a dainty
glass sliper?
Cinderelephant!

Ha! Ha! Ha! Ha! Ha! Ha!

Practice Page 4

Name _____

Use your best handwriting to copy the words.

climb

top

inside

Tip: All uppercase letters should touch the top and bottom lines.

Use your best handwriting to copy the sentences below.

Why did King Kong climb to the top of the Empire State Building? Because he could not fit inside the elevator!

Bonus Chuckle!

What happened when the gorilla ate too much candy?

He got a belly-ape!

Ha! Ha! Ha! Ha! Ha! Ha!

Why Did King Kong
Climb to the top of
the empire state
Building? Because he
Could not fit in
the elevator

Name _____

Use your best handwriting to copy the words.

fish

ocean

goes

Use your best handwriting to copy the sentences below.

What kind of fish lives in the ocean and goes perfectly

with peanut butter?   Jellyfish!

Handwriting Practice: Jokes & Riddles • © 2010 Scholastic • 11

Tip: Lowercase letters b, d, f, h, and l are tall. They all touch the top line.

Ha! • Ha! • Ha! • Ha! • Ha! • Ha! • Ha!

Peanut Butter

Bonus chuckle!

What is the best way to communicate with a fish?

Drop it a line!

Tip: Lowercase letters *g, p, q,* and *y* have tails. The tails hang down below the bottom line.

Name

Use your best handwriting to copy the words.

birds   fly   winter

Use your best handwriting to copy the sentences below.

Why do birds always fly south in the winter?

Because it is way too far for them to walk!

FLORIDA 700 MILES

Ha! • Ha! • Ha! • Ha! • Ha! • Ha! • Ha!

Bonus Chuckle!

What do you give a sick bird?

Tweetment!

Name _____

Use your best handwriting to copy the words.

bear

cross

skunk

Tip: Try to make all of your letters stand up straight.

Use your best handwriting to copy the sentences below.

What do you get when you cross a teddy bear with a skunk?

Winnie the Phew!

Ha! Ha! Ha! Ha! Ha! Ha!

Bonus Chuckle!

What is black and white and goes round and round?

A skunk stuck in a revolving door!

Name _____

Use your best handwriting to copy the words.

pony   say   horse

Use your best handwriting to copy the sentences below.

What did the pony say when he had a sore throat?

"Excuse me, I am a little horse."

Ha! • Ha! • Ha! • Ha! • Ha! • Ha! • Ha! • Ha!

Bonus chuckle!

Where do sick ponies go?

The horse-pital!

Tip: If you are coming to the end of the line, begin the next word on the following line.

Use your best handwriting to copy the words.

sharks   swim   them

Use your best handwriting to copy the sentences below.

Why do sharks swim only in saltwater?

Because pepper makes them sneeze!

ACHOO!

Ha! · Ha! · Ha! · Ha! · Ha! · Ha!

Ha! · Ha! · Ha! · Ha! · Ha!

Bonus Chuckle!

What happened when the shark swallowed a bunch of keys?

He got lockjaw!

Tip: Practice writing your letters in the air.

Name _____

Use your best handwriting to copy the words.

alligator   is   drink

Use your best handwriting to copy the sentences below.

What is an alligator's very favorite thing to drink?

Gatorade, of course!

Ha! • Ha! • Ha! • Ha! • Ha! • Ha! • Ha!

Bonus Chuckle!

What is an alligator always wearing?

Alligator shoes!

Name _____

Use your best handwriting to copy the words.

black   red   white

Tip: You can practice writing your letters in the sand.

Use your best handwriting to copy the sentences below.

What is black and white and red all over!

A very embarrassed zebra!

Ha! • Ha! • Ha! • Ha! • Ha! • Ha! • Ha! •

Bonus Chuckle!

What do zebras have in common with old movies?

They only come in black and white!

Tip: You can practice writing your letters on your friend's back.

Name _____

Use your best handwriting to copy the words.

parrot

say

duck

Use your best handwriting to copy the sentences below.

What did the parrot say when he fell in love with the duck?

"Polly want a quacker!"

Ha! • Ha! • Ha! • Ha! • Ha! • Ha! • Ha! • Ha! • Ha! • Ha!

Bonus Chuckle!

What time does a duck wake up?

The quack of dawn!

Name _____

Use your best handwriting to copy the words.

cows   field   night

Use your best handwriting to copy the sentences below.

Why were Farmer Brown's cows never in the field
on a Saturday evening? That was moo-vie night!

Bonus Chuckle!

Why did the cow cross the road?

To get to the udder side!

POP coRN

Ha! · Ha! · Ha! · Ha! · Ha! · Ha! · Ha!

Tip: You can practice writing your letters with finger paints.

Tip: Drawing circles, squares, and triangles will help you write better letters.

Name _____

Use your best handwriting to copy the words.

snail

world

house

Use your best handwriting to copy the sentences below.

Why is a snail the strongest animal in the world?

No other creature can carry a whole house on its back!

Ha! Ha! Ha! Ha! Ha! Ha! Ha!

Bonus Chuckle!

What did the snail say to the slug with wings?

My, how slime flies!

Name _____

Use your best handwriting to copy the words.

bats   live

hang

Use your best handwriting to copy the sentences below.

Why do bats always live in gigantic groups?

Because they love to hang out with their friends!

Tip: Practice your handwriting a little each day.

Ha! • Ha! • Ha! • Ha! • Ha! • Ha!

Bonus Chuckle!

How did the bat learn to fly?

Batting practice!

Name _____

Use your best handwriting to copy the words.

centipede

parrot

Use your best handwriting to copy the sentences below.

What do you get when you cross a centipede with

a very chatty parrot? A walkie-talkie!

Ha! Ha! Ha! Ha! Ha! Ha! Ha! Ha!

TALK TALK
TALK TALK
TALK
TALK

Bonus Chuckle!

Why was the centipede late for the party?

He decided to put on his shoes!

Name _____

Use your best handwriting to copy the words.

dolphin

cross

tide

Use your best handwriting to copy the sentences below.

Why did the bottlenose dolphin cross the Atlantic Ocean?

To get to the other tide!

Tip: Make sure you have a good eraser before you begin writing.

Ha! Ha! Ha! Ha! Ha! Ha! Ha!

Bonus Chuckle!

How do dolphins make a decision?

Flipper coin!

Name _____

Use your best handwriting to copy the words.

dog

hen

eggs

Use your best handwriting to copy the sentences below.

What do you get when you cross a hen with a hound dog?

Pooched eggs!

Ha! • Ha! • Ha! • Ha! • Ha! • Ha! • Ha!

Tip: A clean desktop is the best place to practice your handwriting.

Bonus Chuckle!

What is the opposite of cock-a-doodle-doo?

A cock-a-doodle-don't!

Name

Use your best handwriting to copy the words.

bees   always   can

Use your best handwriting to copy the sentences below.

Why are bees always humming?

Because they can never remember all of the words!

Ha! • Ha! • Ha! • Ha! • Ha! • Ha! • Ha!

Tip: Always try your very best.

HUMMM

HUMMM

Bonus Chuckle!

What's even more impressive than a talking bird?

A spelling bee!

Name _____

Use your best handwriting to copy the words.

bullfrog

the   he

Use your best handwriting to copy the sentences below.

What happened when the bullfrog broke his leg?

He became very unhoppy!

Tip: Have a good time! Handwriting is fun.

Bonus Chuckle!

What happened to the frog's car?

It got toad away!

Ha! • Ha! • Ha! • Ha! • Ha! • Ha!

Tip: Begin letters from the top, not the bottom.

Name _____

Use your best handwriting to copy the words.

do   porcupine   turtle

Use your best handwriting to copy the sentences below.

What do you get when you cross a porcupine with a turtle?

A real slowpoke!

Ha! • Ha! • Ha! • Ha! • Ha! • Ha! • Ha! • Ha!

Bonus Chuckle!

How do turtles communicate with other turtles?

Shell phones!

Name _____

Use your best handwriting to copy the words.

butterfly

to   was

Use your best handwriting to copy the sentences below.

Why wasn't the butterfly invited to the dance?

Because the dance was a moth-ball!

Tip: Pull the pencil toward the middle of your body when you write.

MOTH BALL

Why did the little boy throw butter out the window?

He wanted to see the butter fly!

Ha! Ha! Ha! Ha! Ha! Ha! Ha!

Name

Use your best handwriting to copy the words.

rhino

phone

two

Use your best handwriting to copy the sentences below.

What is harder than getting a rhino into a phone booth?

Getting two rhinos into a phone booth!

Tip: Use your pinkie finger or a paper clip to measure the space between each word.

Ha! • Ha! • Ha! • Ha! • Ha! • Ha! • Ha!

Bonus Chuckle!

What should you do if you see a blue rhino?

Cheer it up!

Name _____

Use your best handwriting to copy the words.

girl

oil

mouse

Tip: All uppercase letters should touch the top and bottom lines.

Use your best handwriting to copy the sentences below.

Why did the little girl pour oil on her new pet mouse?

Because it was squeaking!

Bonus chuckle!

What game does every mouse love to play?

Hide and squeak!

Name _____

Use your best handwriting to copy the words.

mosquito   go

bite

Use your best handwriting to copy the sentences below.

Why did the mosquito go to see the dentist?

He wanted to improve his bite!

Ha! • Ha! • Ha! • Ha! • Ha! • Ha!

DENTIST

Tip:
Lowercase
letters *b, d, f, h,*
and *l* are tall.
They all touch
the top line.

Bonus Chuckle!

What do you
get when
you cross a
mosquito and
a snowman?

Frostbite!

Tip: Lowercase letters *g, p, q,* and *y* have tails. The tails hang down below the bottom line.

Name _____

Use your best handwriting to copy the words.

pig   home

school

Use your best handwriting to copy the sentences below.

Why did the little pig go straight home after school?

He had lots and lots of ham-work to do!

Ha! • Ha! • Ha! • Ha! • Ha! • Ha! • Ha!

**Bonus
chuckle!**

**Where did the
pioneer keep
his pigs?**

In a hog cabin!

Name

Use your best handwriting to copy the words.

chicken

get

slide

Use your best handwriting to copy the sentences below.

Why did the chicken cross the playground?

He wanted to get to the other slide!

Tip: Try to make all of your letters stand up straight.

Ha! Ha! Ha! Ha! Ha! Ha!

Bonus Chuckle!

What do you call a funny book for chickens?

A yolk book!

Practice Page
28

Tip: Always take your time when practicing your handwriting.

Name _____

Use your best handwriting to copy the words.

ant

great

uncle

Use your best handwriting to copy the sentences below.

What do you call an ant that lives with your great uncle?

Your great ant of course!

Ha! Ha! Ha! Ha! Ha! Ha! Ha!

Bonus chuckle!

Where do ants like to go on vacation?

Fr-ants!

Name _____

Use your best handwriting to copy the words.

worm   apple   half

Use your best handwriting to copy the sentences below.

What is the only thing worse than finding a worm
in your apple?   Finding half a worm in your apple!

Tip: If you are coming to the end of the line, begin the next word on the following line.

Ha! Ha! Ha! Ha! Ha! Ha! Ha!

Tip: You can practice writing your letters in the air.

Name _____

Use your best handwriting to copy the words.

rabbit

whole

wide

Use your best handwriting to copy the sentences below.

Who is the strongest rabbit in the whole wide world?

Hare-cules!

Ha! Ha! Ha! Ha! Ha! Ha! Ha!

Bonus Chuckle!

What is a rabbit's favorite dance style?

Hip-hop!

Name _____

Use your best handwriting to copy the words.

fly

between

bird

Use your best handwriting to copy the sentences below.

What is the difference between a fly and a bird?

A bird can fly but a fly cannot bird!

Tip: You can practice writing your letters in the sand.

Ha! Ha! Ha! Ha! Ha! Ha! Ha!

Bonus chuckle!

Why did the fly fly?

Because the spider spied 'er!

Name _____

Use your best handwriting to copy the words.

owl

voice

hoot

Tip: You can practice writing your letters on your friend's back.

Use your best handwriting to copy the sentences below.

What happened when the owl lost his voice?

Nothing, because he did not give a hoot!

Ha! Ha! Ha! Ha! Ha! Ha! Ha! Ha!

Bonus chuckle!

What is green and loves to peck at trees?

Woody Wood-pickle!

Name _____

Use your best handwriting to copy the words.

turkey

prove

not

Use your best handwriting to copy the sentences below.

Why did the turkey decide to skydive?

He had to prove that he was not chicken!

Tip: You can practice writing your letters with finger paints.

Ha! Ha! Ha! Ha! Ha! Ha! Ha!

Bonus Chuckle!

What is a turkey's favorite dessert?

Peach gobbler!

Name _____

Use your best handwriting to copy the words.

snakes

funny

joke

Use your best handwriting to copy the sentences below.

What do snakes say when they hear a very funny joke?

"That was so hiss-terical!"

Ha! Ha! Ha! Ha! Ha! Ha! Ha! Ha! Ha!

HA! HA! HA! HA!

Tip: Drawing circles, squares, and triangles will help you write better letters.

Bonus Chuckle!

What is a snake's favorite subject in school?

Hiss-story!

Name

Use your best handwriting to copy the words.

leopard   in   long

Use your best handwriting to copy the sentences below.

Did you hear what happened to the leopard who

stayed in the shower too long?   He became spotless!

Tip: Practice your handwriting a little each day.

Ha!   Ha!   Ha!   Ha!   Ha!   Ha!   Ha!   Ha!   Ha!

Bonus Chuckle!

What is the difference between a tiger and a lion?

A tiger has the mane part missing!

Name _____

Use your best handwriting to copy the words.

giraffe   for   school

Use your best handwriting to copy the sentences below.

Why was the little giraffe late for school?

Because his mom got stuck in a huge giraffic jam!

HONK! HONK!

Bonus Chuckle!

What do giraffes have that no other animal has?

Baby giraffes!

Ha! • Ha! • Ha! • Ha! • Ha! • Ha!

Name _____

Practice Page 37

Tip: Make sure you have a good eraser before you begin writing.

Use your best handwriting to copy the words.

kangaroo   to   see

Use your best handwriting to copy the sentences below.

Why did the kangaroo hop over to see his doctor?

He was feeling quite jumpy!

DR. WOMBAT

Ha! • Ha! • Ha! • Ha! • Ha! • Ha! • Ha! •

Bonus Chuckle!

What is a kangaroo's favorite season?

Spring!

Tip: A clean desktop is the best place to practice your handwriting.

Name _____

Use your best handwriting to copy the words.

little

say

penguin

Use your best handwriting to copy the sentences below.

What did the ocean say to the little penguin?

Nothing. It just waved!

Ha! Ha! Ha! Ha! Ha! Ha! Ha! Ha!

Bonus Chuckle!

What is a penguin's favorite drink?

A waddle bottle!

Name

Use your best handwriting to copy the words.

spider   did

crawl

Use your best handwriting to copy the sentences below.

Why did the spider crawl across the computer keyboard?

He wanted to make a Web site!

Handwriting Practice: Jokes & Riddles • © 2010 Scholastic • 45

Tip: Always try your very best.

Ha! Ha! Ha! Ha! Ha! Ha! Ha!

Bonus Chuckle!

Why did the spider buy a car?

He wanted to go for a spin!

Tip: Have a good time! Handwriting is fun.

Name _____

Use your best handwriting to copy the words.

grizzly

bear

rain

Use your best handwriting to copy the sentences below.

What do you call a grizzly bear that gets caught in the rain?

A drizzly bear!

Ha! • Ha! • Ha! • Ha! • Ha! • Ha! • Ha!

Bonus Chuckle!

What is a polar bear's very favorite food?

A brrr-grrr!

Blank Booklet Page

Photocopy this page and cut along the dashed line to make an additional booklet page.

Booklet Cover

Photocopy this page and cut along the dashed line to make a booklet cover.

Animal Jokes & Riddles

With handwriting by

HA! HA! HA! HA!

HA! HA! HA! HA!